PRAISE

for *I PRAY ANYWAY*

D0167900

"In *I Pray Anyway*, Joyce Wilson-Sanford shares with us a compilation of honest reflections that will resonate with anyone who finds oneself in the 'messy middle' when it comes to prayer and religion. Although you might well end up with more than one of Joyce's insightful prayers taped to your bathroom mirror, there is an even greater gift that emerges from her collection as a whole—the inspiration to explore prayer even if you remain restless and uncertain about your relationship to organized religion."

E.S.

Professor of Biology

"If you have ever struggled with the institutions of religion yet always felt there is something bigger in life, read this book! It is a beautiful journey in a simple format of short prayers—unlike what you may assume—with a life story woven in. It can be savored, read a page a day, or devoured but either way it's a great read. It allows one to reflect on your own personal journey, and what the heck...Pray Anyway!"

SCOTT HARRISON

Business Executive

"With enormous wit and wisdom, Joyce Wilson-Sanford lays bare her own struggles and stumbles in the process of developing a satisfying spiritual life, and in so doing gives everyone else permission to stumble. All in all, this is a truly refreshing read. Anyone tackling it will feel as though they are being asked to attend a Come as You Are Party – which is the oldest and most trustworthy spiritual invitation."

(THE REV.) MARY CUSHMAN

"You might be ambivalent about prayer, but you'll experience no ambivalence about Wilson-Sanford's warmth, hope, humor…and wisdom."

VICTORIA ZACKHEIM

Author of Faith: Essays from Believers, Agnostics, and Atheists

"Equally accessible to believers and skeptics, I Pray Anyway left me both smiling and sighing in understanding and recognition of the human experience so aptly captured in Joyce's prayers."

KATHERINE CAULEY, PHD

Vice Chair and Professor, Department of Community Health
Wright State University

"This book is a beautiful bridge for all those who feel that prayer, God and the spiritual realm is way out there somewhere. Joyce Wilson-Sanford brings 'prayer' home to daily life, ongoing wrestlings and ultimately growth. It is authentic, humble, and full of mundane grit, a personal journal of her humanity and vulnerability as a seeker. I have used some of the prayers in teaching my Spirituality class. Everyone responds, because she speaks to us all!"

SUSAN HOWE

Chaplain

"This is a lovely book—Joyce is open and vulnerable with her personal experience of prayer. She invites the reader to find his or her own way to communicate with the Divine. I am not yet where she is, and I may not get to the same place as she does, but it is good to have some hidebound assumptions questioned. Her example in this book helped me to consider doing that. I remain ambivalent, but less alone."

DR. ANTHONY MCCANN, MD

Doctor of Psychiatry

"I thumbed to a page in I Pray Anyway, holding space to see whether this is a true book of assistance and guidance. My eyes landed, focused and read—one devotion will do—I am completely taken by the timeliness of the message and the spirit of action it invoked in me. This is not a book, but a wise and patient friend."

THOMAS FURBER

Business Executive

I pray anyway

DEVOTIONS FOR THE AMBIVALENT

JOYCE
WILSON-SANFORD

RED SHOE PRESS

Copyright ©2016 by Joyce Wilson-Sanford

Published by Red Shoe Press

All rights reserved

ISBN:
978-0-9863386-0-1

Cover & Book Design:
Perch Design Studio

To those of us that can't hold on,
but won't let go —

ABOUT THIS BOOK

This book
Started with my prayers
After years of none
I wrote some down
As a way to hear myself
My daughter peeked
Was touched
The title grabbed me
I shared it
People laughed
Then clapped
Then said—Oh, I need this book,
I'm hungry, I'm searching,
Ambivalence wears me out
I said—I know,
That's why I decided
To pray anyway

Here "I" am: this patchwork, this bundle of questions and doubt and obsessions, this gravitation to silence and to the woods and to love. This incoherence!

THOMAS MERTON

Your sacred space is where you can find yourself again and again.

JOSEPH CAMPBELL

AMBIVALENCE

1: simultaneous and contradictory attitudes or feelings (as attraction and repulsion) toward an object, person, or action

2 a: continual fluctuation (as between one thing and its opposite)
b: uncertainty as to which approach to follow

MERRIAM-WEBSTER

FOREWORD

Is the sky falling?
Has it always been falling?
No idea
But I can feel things shifting
We are the in-betweens
Old forms disintegrating
No new ones yet
Transformation starting with chaos
Organized religion has to
disorganize
Find new forms
New integrity
New spirit
So, we are unwilling pioneers
In this new shared
Fluid spiritual hunger

I had my first spiritual inkling –

—in fourth grade Sunday School
Mrs. Selye was my teacher
She inspired me
I decided to be a missionary
She gave us all a Bible
The New Standard Revised Edition
It was maroon and looked like a book not a Bible'
Mrs. Selye did the unthinkable
She taught us how to write in our Bibles
Permission to underline
I was a bookworm
I read that book cover to cover
Stumbling determinedly
Through all the names and generations
I was fervent until sixth grade
When I put 2 and 2 together and rejected God
Got mad at God
Good and mad

/

Waking up to joy
Is sometimes easy
Like sliding into your slippers
Other days it takes discipline
Like dreaded sit-ups
Still, joy should be
The only option
For a new day

2

Let great big wonderful things be possible
Let's quit dumbing down our hope
Why not why not why not wonderful?
Step me into free fall
Take my breath away
Let's have marvels
Miracles
We are at that point
The impossible is mandatory

3

Beauty
I sit in it, but refuse to soften
I look again
Here is glory
A single blossom does it
How was I immune a moment ago?
Wake-up

A pedicure blocked my prayer
Needing one
Wanting one
Wondering if I could have one today
Over and over
A pedicure?
Blocking sweetness
Blocking comfort
Blocking love for others
A pedicure!

I take any path
Hindu
Sufi
Christian
Jewish
I walk until a clearing opens
Then I stop
The paths go on and on
I continue

Hard not to see you as a person
You who are formless
You who are
Spirit?
Energy?
Connection among hearts?
Force for good?
The universal ocean we swim in?
You are so not a person
Awesome and unknowable

7

Joy is a by-product
Of peace with what is
Happiness comes and goes
A joyride lasts forever

I've been gone so long
So busy living
Birthing, burying, caring
Off-center
Avoiding the stillness
Uncomfortable
Feeling restless
Itchy
Artificial
Hypocritical
So many ways to keep myself away
So I force myself
Holding
Holding
Here again
Trying again

9

I get hungry
My appetite is huge
I consume the wrong things
Food shoes books
Stuff
Then I feed myself some silence
Some devotion
Some nothingness
And I am full

10

I hate wallowing in my
Crazy stuff
It's so wasteful
So unkind to me
Pulling my feet out
Of the crazy glue
That sticks me
To all that gunk
Is beyond me

11

Tonight my prayer is tender
Shy
I am bashful
Wanting to step forward into belief
But straddling
An untenable position
Uncomfortable
Unsustainable
And yet
I'm shy, embarrassed
To step forward with both feet
Been straddling for so long
If I take a step
I might fall over

I can be blind to my own abundance
It can hurt others
It can create distance
It can humiliate
Even while I share

13

A dentist-drill-morning from across the street
Cars needing help
New parts
Scraping
Now light tapping
Rust removal
Then ready to roll
Just like a soul repair shop

14

So full of me
I need to whirl
Like a dervish
Until me is overwhelmed
And I disappear
Tough old ego

15

My heart cracks open
Flops like a filleted fish
Insides exposed
Contained pain
Burst the seams
Of my heart
That wants to love again

16

Be quiet me
This is for others
For hurting countries
For inadequate leaders
For hungry bellies
For unloved people
For the violence-addicted
For bodies fading
For shriveled souls
For pain bearers
For us all

17

So many people thinking they are right
Knowing truth about mystery
Trying to lock it down their way
Mystery won't have it
So why not just
Know the 'not knowing'
Be sure of that

18

I pray wrong and frustrated
Eyes squeezed shut
Can't make it work
My neck is stiff
My mind buzzes
I work too hard
I can't settle into prayer
I give up
Just show up

19

I am known for a kind of joy
Nothing makes me happier than a rule well broken
Just a little naughtiness makes my day
And so I don't act my age
Mainly because I don't know it
But I've decided to let myself get older
More deep peace
More forgiveness
More letting go of achievement
More noodling on the miracles
But I will always dance in the kitchen
And break a rule that needs it

20

God
So many thanks
So many
Allowing you to be possible
Makes life more interesting
And hopeful
What's next?

21

Some of my prayer
Can get phony
I push for peace
When I need to express
The fear or rage or sorrow
Nagging to be relieved
Thank goodness
My dark side is a nag

22

Sour and cynical
I force myself to devotions
Who cares?
Guess I do
Cause here I am
Grumpy
Determined not to be comforted
Dedicated to being unhappy
All wrong
One black-eyed Susan settles me down
It's just that today
Life hurts

23

Action or distraction is where I live
Rarely holding still
Enough
To be in peace
To align with harmony
Out of time
Is where I am
Timelessness is what I want

24

Why not believe?
Or live like you believe?
What's the loss?
Compared to the gain?
More hope
More fun and adventure
More mystery
More guidance
More purpose
Why not believe?

25

Ego keeps knocking at my door
Even in prayer
Tickling me with ideas about me
Poor hard-working ego
Takes awhile to feel safe
Ego finally fades
Eased of that burden
Prayerfulness comes
Comfort and joy

26

Soft heart
Soft belly
Sadness emerges
Joy follows
Sweet pain
Not fun
But true

27

Am I talking to you?
Or am I talking to me?
My best me, but me?
Does it matter?
Yes
And no

28

Death has been chasing my tail
And I've been running
Give me the courage to turn around
Embrace it
Walk with it
No need to run
Make friends
Walk leisurely

29

Greedy Greedy Greedy
Needy Needy Needy
Gimme Gimme Gimme
Want it Want it Want it
The Wheel of Want
Give me a break

30

Oh, the divine is funny
I arrange for uninterrupted devotion time
Morning
Before words and tasks
Broken fridge
My husband is frantic about rotten food
He knocks
The choice is clear
And irritating
Pure clean love
Or everyday dirty love
Rotten cabbage
Here I come

3/

I read
Wanting to know
To validate my experience
To split theological hairs
To find words to relieve my doubt
To support my cowardice
I shut the books
I pray anyway

I PRAY ANYWAY

In sixth grade,
I gave up God—

—on Christmas Eve no less

Went to Christmas Eve service with my mom and dad, college brother and his fiancé

My best friend, Jan, and I were in the choir

We went to her house after service for Polish food and festivities

Couldn't wait to tell her I had been kissed for the first time

My boy crush and later love had come by my house with mistletoe that day

And used it—yuck and yoweee

I remember red-hot cheeks from one little peck

I never told Jan about the kiss

A phone call ruined Christmas and God for me

My brother's fiancé's family had been killed in a car accident

Hit by a drunken driver

Her grandparents, her parents, her seven-year-old brother and a new baby girl

Her nine-year-old sister lived
So many ramifications from that night
I did not have an alcoholic drink until I was
forty-four years old
I refused church, Sunday school, prayer, Bible
If God was not good, phooey on him
Done
For quite a while
I gave up God

32

I invite my parts to the table
We need to talk
Ms. Shame
Ferocious Mama
Lousy Spouse
Greedy Doll
Madam Ego
Stinky Friend
Lazy Loser
Fat 'n Ugly
You are not as bad as you imagine
Forget about yourself
Go do some good

33

Here I am
Wrestling with the devil
I know that church scared me today
Too loud, too sure of itself
So here I am at the kitchen table
Finding God in the mundane silence

34

Listening
Heart and mind
Letting it all just be
Some excitement
An inkling of ringing true
More listening
Just listening
Letting things ripen

35

I have someone who is a sliver in my soul
My efforts do nothing
I give up
I give in
What's the story?
More lessons to come?
Well, bring it on
Bring resolution
Even the peace of defeat is OK
There I go again
Doing the guiding
Lesson accomplished

36

Back to joy
Recuperation
Back to love
For all and everything
Laughter lives here
Compassion too
Let's see how long I carry it with me today

37

Heal my broken mother's heart
My heart
My mother's heart
Her mother's heart
The hearts of mothers
Broken at birth
Healing as we love—open and broken
Come in

38

Sometimes I get Old Testament willies
Afraid of retribution
Wanting to be good in order to get
Have to calm myself
Trust
I'm not in charge
Not that important
I refrain from imploring
Back to gratitude
For the imperfect perfect
Just as I am
Just as it is

39

Oops, almost forgot God
To play computer games
To read in bed
To make my list of things to do
To luxuriate
To text my kids
Just too busy, for 'goodness' sake

40

Praying with coffee jitters
Jittering away
Reaching for calm
Too far to reach
Enough is enough
Peace is not of time
And I am locked in time right now

41

I can be so nasty
Negative, sarcastic
Feels lousy actually
I do so love to be superior
I want to call back these words
Don't want to pick on me either
Just accept

42

I am so flawed
My ego loves to dance
It hits me hard
Then I pause
Get hit by my own human foibles
What a mess
Now I laugh
I'm not that important
What a relief

43

Which comes first chicken or egg?
Faith first, then God?
God first, then faith?
Like playing chicken
You first
No
You first
You can't strain to faith

44

I pray for every person on this globe
To move a micro-measure more
Toward compassion
Receive it
Give it
Create conditions for it
Baby steps to peace
Accumulating

In here
Is joy
The ember
Steady and warm
Out there is
Well—
What is
Leave what is
Come on in
Out of the cold

46

Bless my children
Soothe hurts I've brought to them
Revel in them like I do
Call forth their good
Guide them to their tasks
Fortify them
Allow them great joy
Bless my children

47

Have I forgotten gratitude?
I know I have
I save it for what I want
Not for what I have
Dumb ingratitude
Dumb dumb dumb
So now thanks
Soul-deep grateful

48

Into the pool of sorrow I go
Descending past pain
Deeper into the clear water
I hold
Then push up
Into joy again
But I dread the descent
Still wanting joy without pain

49

Oh no, that's too exciting
I'll tamp down that idea
Make it manageable
Talk myself out of it
Be realistic
Or
Pull my courage out of storage
Not be a spiritual coward

50

Works every time
But every time is the first time
Down in the dumps?
Sad about bumps in your precious road?
Luxurious anxiety, not the survival kind?
Give, create, connect
Bingo!
Try a little learning

Wow wow wow wow wow
Anxious
Racing heart
All chaos
Overwhelmed with
Fear actually
Life won't last
Can make you shake sometimes

52

Fall away friends
Fall away hopes for children
Fall away goals, accomplishment
Fall away body
Fall away dear ego
Fall away fall away
Fall away all

53

I'm here
Stepping into peace
Each breath deeper as I enter
My hurts sharper but soothed too
I slow down—enter both the pain and sorrow
Transforming it to something sweet
My heart hurts and here I am
Sitting with it all
At last, being no one going nowhere
If just for a moment

54

Sick sick sick
Of it
From it
Body brain soul
Sometimes it all just goes to hell
So easy to stay there
Sometimes I have to crawl to peace
Shedding disgust as I go

I want a clean heart
I breathe deep
Down and deep
Hurtful peace
Peaceful hurt
Breathing down
Cleaning out the corners
Of my heart

56

Celebrating a miracle
Cautiously
Quietly
Too quick to downgrade it
Calling it luck
No
A miracle

57

Forget zeal
Zeal is crazy making
Try prudence
Steadfastness
Tolerance
Love when it's tough
Grounded
Rooted
Patient
Quiet
Faith in things unseen

58

Thank you thank you thank you
For this sharp, sun-lit winter day
For all the comforts I have
Books
Beauty
Plenty of people to love
Fun food to cook
Words to write
Possibilities to grow
Incredibly blessed
And for one glorious moment
I know it
With no equivocation

59

Arguing today
Battling theologians
Only my experience holds steady
I pray anyway
Steady even with my doubt
Flailing all the way
Praying anyway

Boys brought me
back to church,
but not to—

—God

And not to the same church

Only as I write, do I realize I never again stepped foot in my childhood church

But I did cut across the alley to the EUB church

Evangelical United Brethren Church

(Very different from my mild Methodist church)

Where kids hung out

Where we tolerated embarrassing activities just to be close to our common, thundering hormones

I roller-skated, I sang Christmas carols, I collected clothing, I served soup

I dressed up fit to kill in honor of those hormones for every Sunday School class

God played no part in this church going

60

Coffee is the great comforter
There in time of need
Sip—Sigh—Sip
Coffee is a connector
Come in, I'll make coffee
Coffee restores
A big slurp keeps us going
Coffee energizes
Creates buzz
It warms and holds and prepares
It accompanies tough moments of loss
It's hearty
Coffee stains are gorgeous, unique
Not a wrong thing
We spill
We stain
Life's a mess
A joyous mess
Come on in
Let's laugh

61

Ouch
Families can hurt
Ouch
Fold or strike back
Neither
Just dig down to more love
I'm digging
Trust me

62

The stunned gratitude
As winter people come into the sun
Cautious to believe the reprieve
And then slow smiles as they trust
Spring
Rebirth
Hope
Such a vulnerability
This faith
Because winter will come again
Count on it
Bless our sweet selves

63

What should I do about this?
What should I do about that?
Am I right?
Am I wrong?
Wobble wobble wobble
Frantically working to make it all work
Let go of fixing
Kids
Money
Relationships
Myself
Work
Life purpose (really? how grandiose!)
Shut up
Be

64

I've been touched by miracles
Still a lost earring can ruin my day
Really??
Really

65

Mighty
Wow
To think of Might
Mighty
Powerful
Forceful
Awesome
Again and again
I forget about the possibility of invisible forces
I am relieved
I want more than me

66

Flopping around in old memories
Regrets
If only—
Darn
If only I'd get over myself
Help someone else get out of their own way
Both of us better for it
Self-centered so doesn't work long term

67

Blessings blessings blessings
On all my others
My husband
My children
Their children
My brother-in-law
My sister-in-law
My nephews
My cousins
My friends
All I know
All my dead
Blessings
Blessings
Blessings

68

I could stay here forever
There—I've ruined it!!!!

69

Ok
Gratitude
Everything sucks, but I'll do gratitude
Watch me now
Thanks (Grrrrrrrr)
I'm so blessed! (Ri-ight)
Ok
Let me count the ways
Just counted five
Big ones
Five more
Like sit-ups
And embarrassingly enough
I am better
The negative hysteria is at bay
Whew
Perspective
Put me right side up

70

Churning
Why do I care about divine stuff?
Superstition?
Tradition?
Lack of courage?
Can't I just be a person doing my best?
What's 'the more' that I want?
That I won't accept anyway
Churn churn churn

71

I am not modern
I believe in wrongness
Sin is just another ruined word
But wrong exists
I want the fixing of wrong to be hard
A spiritual balancing scale

72

Wrestling
With my self-centeredness
My ability to sting back when stung
On the backside of my ego
It roars like a bear
And launches like an arrow
Attacking
Wanting to win
I want to win over wanting to win
Life lessons are sooooo funny

73

Joy is there waiting
In the silence and solitude
My cup of coffee hot
My cup of hope
My everyday chalice

74

How do people suffer
Without hope
Without faith
Without being held?
I can't do it
I need belief in something more
I am not strong enough alone
And I am plenty strong

75

Here's the impossible part
To say 'your will'
Whoever
Whatever
I want 'my will'
And to fake surrender
While having it my way
Doesn't work that way, I know
Life is one big surrender

76

Giddy with possibilities!
Let the giddiness go
Stay with the possibilities
Everything isn't
A miracle

77

I'm hurting from a skirmish
Trying not to be dedicated to being right
But having said too many words already
Wanting to sow peace but to be vindicated
My words were too strong
Looking for peace and harmony a little late
Shutting up might be good
Let night do its work

78

Coming back to prayer
Feels like
Going to sleep
In my childhood bed
As an adult
Made ready by loving parents
Familiar and safe
And strange
At the same time

79

With a proofreader's eye
I can find the one thing wrong
With anything
Scanning for
The out of place
The must get done
The needing repair
Shifting my focus to the good
Is like separating magnets

80

I come for peace
Sometimes it's there for me
Sometimes not
Why does one time make me distrust the other?
This need for absolute something or other
Is the issue
My absolute?
Keep coming

81

I am sitting on top of fury
An injustice done over time
Makes me fume
A slow burn volcano
Surface forgiveness won't hold
Digging deeper
Will produce hot lava
Deep forgiveness?
Must I?
Can I?
Will I?
I'd rather read

82

Spoiled brat-ness
I am covered with it
Grateful but not generous enough
My giving circle is too small
Only people I know and like
I need to stretch me
Beyond me
To people I don't know
People I can't stand
People I just don't get
People who hurt me
The world can't afford spoiled brats

83

What a burden
To think that only your thoughts
Create your reality
And leave out
The possibility
Of spiritual support
I'd rather ride shotgun

84

I didn't expect so much heartbreak
From family
The supposed safe place
I'd like to join the numbed out
But too late for me
Religion may be an opiate
But prayer isn't
Not a pain reliever but
A clarifier

85

No prayer tonight
Just thrashing
Lashing out at my own distractions
Too busy being mad at me
Can't join
Or surrender
Or rest
A bust tonight
Oh well
More to come

86

Right now
I am ambivalent about my ambivalence
Or sharing my ambivalence
It's tiresome
Embarrassing
Maybe cowardly
But it would be a lie to resolve it
Toward pure doubt
Or pure faith
The messy middle
Is my experience

87

Prayer for others is so satisfying
Who knows the invisible connections?
Such natural easy prayer
Wanting good for those I love
Now to pray for those I don't

88

I have loaded up on words
Reading reading reading
Reading
Reading
Reading
Packing down my pain
Like brown sugar
In a cup
Using words
To beat me into oblivion
To press my anguish into
Something with form

89

I cringe
My 'sins' are not intangible
Do I take what is not mine?
Do I lie for convenience?
Do I position myself to look good?
Do I always want more?
Let me count the ways

90

It's awkward to say
"I pray"
I expect quiet tolerance
A kind of pity
For my self-deception
Or subtle separation
From friends
Who wonder
What's going on with me
Saying I pray
Highlights
Not belonging anywhere
Loneliness?
Not quite
A church-goer?
Not quite
A naysayer?
Not quite
I pray anyway

My early teen-age God dry spell ended with falling in love—

—age sixteen
Radiant brilliant glowing falling-in-love-love
The world glistened
So full of gratitude, I re-opened my Bible
New Testament
Love—love—love
Everywhere
Jesus made sense to me
I had so much fullness, so easy to give
So easy to be joyful
I read and discovered theology
Through my now seminary student brother
(Another Christmas Eve ramification)
I gave up the EUB church
(found my boyfriend)
Still I did nightly devotions
Enjoyed prayer
God was good againt

91

A good day
A perfect day
Left me digging
For something to complain about
I found it too
But, I won't have it
I had a perfect day
Laughter
Beauty
Intimacy
Music
Food
Friends
No complaining allowed
Nope
Won't do it
I had a perfect day

92

I flubbed up today
A cringer
A humdinger of embarrassment
It ruins my prayer
Since when am I so important?
I was a doofus
Now what?
A thousand apologies?
I don't matter that much
Getting it right
Getting it wrong
Still just me

93

I hang onto my ambivalence
For dear life
Or at least for life as I have it now
Feeling the slip and slide
Into a new stance
That I resist

94

My Birthday
I have been given to and given to
And given to
Basking in generosity
I sit
And receive
Grateful
Safe with those I love
And who love me
I won't bat this away
But enjoy the gift

"Be still and know that I am God"
What else is there to say?
Thanks

96

Wrestling with the devil and the divine both today
Just give me science
Just give me kind people
Just give me a compassionate world
Just give me food for the hungry
Just give me my friends and my family
Good enough jobs for all
What else is needed?
That is the question

97

Today
All about others
Holding them
Listing people until I'm empty
No rhyme or reason
Naming them for blessings
Just to get rid of me
I name them and move on
Side stepping me

98

No prayer for five days
Now I am hungry for it
Have cleared space for it
Fought for space for it
Negotiated the time for it
So I enter jangled
But here I am
Settling in
—Not so fast—
Interrupted by 'in your-face' life
A workman and my husband wanting to check plumbing
Chit-chat chit-chat
Which is better
Patience with people or prayer?
I know
I know
Both

99

Second guessing everything today
Watching myself pray
Rather than praying
Making fun of myself
Doubting and jabbing
Get behind me, Monkey Mind
Shut up, Words
It's my experience, so I'll have it

100

Sometimes if I'm not careful
My prayer spills into superstition
Prayer against fear
Or thinking my thoughts are in charge
Manifesting my craziness
That is the exact time to surrender
Control is the enemy

101

Today is mine to mend
I betrayed me
Pretending an obligation
Was a gift
It wasn't
A martyr?
No, I refuse to enjoy my suffering
Just a mistake
A big fat mistake

102

I feel sorry for me
I just do
In this chipper dipper culture
I just want a minute to feel bad for me
That's hard to sit with
Forbidden
Too bad
Life has hard stuff in it

103

I tried to be a fervent atheist
Found it liberating for awhile
Mostly fun to shock or irritate people
Could not sustain it
Felt false
But cleared space
For a real choice
Now I'm a evangelical agnostic
Wanting to be an everyday mystic

104

I begin my day
It ought to be a good one
Only things in it that I want to do
My space to fill
But rather than luxuriate in it
I'm distracted by buzzing thoughts
Vague yearning
I'm ruining my 'just right' day

105

The death of a loved one
Seems like it should never heal
But it will
Betrayal by betrayal
As life wins
Healing happens
Seems impossible
Wrong even
But why not?
Joy over sorrow
Is a better honoring

106

I've been nervous
(Old fashioned word)
Lately
About dying
Not the dying part
But the living
Am I?

107

Oops
I've gone petty
Catty
Mean-spirited
Sour
Time out for me
Sent to my room
To shut up
Stop
Soften
Blessing on those who receive my ire
For my sake, not theirs

108

It's so easy to forget a miracle
It joins the day-to-day so fast
Then back to yearning all over again
Maybe numbed out is the way it has to be
Or we'd be overtaken by grandeur
We'd explode with wonder and gratitude
Just 'pop' and disintegrate with joy

109

Praying
Makes life more interesting
What will be there today?
Like opening email
What will emerge?
It's not empty meditation
It's fullness
And not just of self
Prayer takes you
To a dialogue without words

110

So easy to slide away
From contemplation on an average day
Bad times make everyone pray in some way
Good times produce gratitude
Day to day
We droop
Drop out of the need and miss
What could be

111

I pray to God
Any other name makes me cringe
Or giggle
Trying too hard to invent
The naming doesn't matter
Took me lots of years to know that
I need to pray 'to'
Or 'talk with' the idea of someone
I am NOT talking to myself
Not even my higher self
But to God-ness
Could care less about names
There are so many
It's the prayer that matters
The praying

112

Prayer will indeed take you there
But who wants to go?
It's not all peace and joy
True is not always easy

113

Help me give up words
Scanning
Book to book
For truth
Solace
Joy
Guidance
Help me step out
Into the free fall
Of silence

114

Waiting for new direction
With a nudge here
A nudge there
With a new person, a new book
With an urge to do something
With a sense of rightness
With goose pimples
With sudden ease of action
With ringing true
With energy to act

115

As I end my prayers
My mystery book calls
Too impatient for the listening part of prayer
The payoff
Knowing it's dumb
I continue to sit
Ready to receive—
Sort of
Trying to be ready
I hear my hunger growls
My need to go to the bathroom
Birds
Groceries that need to be bought
Oh, now I get it
I was expecting something grandiose
Instead
Keep on keep on keep on

116

I am not praying anyway
I'm just not praying at all
Giving up?
Giving in?
Funny, coming to prayer
To not pray

117

I'm tired
Been doing tough generosity
Meaning 'not fun'
Stretching when on empty
Wanting a deeper reservoir of good will
Digging one more time
To find something more to give
Without being nasty
There's the rub

118

Feel gunky today
Spiritually cranky
Need for retreat
Contemplation
Get that spiritual spine aligned again
Neglect of self and sacred
Makes for gunk
Clean me out
Get me ready for more

119

Yearning is a clue
My ego desires
My heart wants
My greed needs
My body craves
Only my soul yearns

120

I'm capable of an underground meanness
Spiteful
Caustic—
And funny
A dark comic dialogue
Playing in my ear
Coming out my mouth
Surprising me
Hurting anyone in the path
Bile hidden in humor
Hateful
Even to myself
Ms. Book About Prayer
Ms. Pray Anyway
Ms. Rather Be Reading A Good Book
Ms. Sailor Mouth
Ms. McMeany

God stayed good
and I stayed devout—

—all through college
I went to church and Wednesday night Communion in a small historic log cabin—regularly
My first roommate was nervous when she saw a Bible on my desk
She was relieved when she saw that I dated
(Every night)
I fell in and out of love with nice guys every semester
Midwest wholesome love
I took a History of Experimental Psychology course
The professor said,—You've too good a brain to believe in God. Hope this course knocks it out of you—
It made a dent
My senior year I got engaged at Christmas and married in June, after graduation
To one of the nice guys
Went into the Peace Corps (a missionary at last)
Then put my husband through law school as a teacher

Young married life
Two children, no church, some prayer,
God diffuse and slightly scorned as not sophisticated
Life for a re-emergence

121

Opening the heart hurts
All that fear
All that vulnerability
Sorrow
Anger
The purge
Leaving such tenderness
And joy
That could have been lost

122

Get me ready
Something big is coming
I am so not ready
Can't I hide some more?
Just enjoy?
Do I hear the universe laugh?
Ha-Ha-Ha
Ha Ha!

123

My heart throws off happiness sparks
Anticipation
Not having yet
But preparing for
Something wonderful
Expectations can be fun
Just don't take them too seriously

124

I have sand in my soul
A constant discomfort
I wrestle to find peace with a loved one
That I often don't like
And then don't like that I don't like
I want to be cleared of the gnawing irritation
It stinks up my day
Like smog
Soul smog
I want to clean my soul filter

125

Today I balked
Just couldn't get settled
Hated everything I did while smiling
Hated everything anyone else did
While still smiling
A sullied day
No prayer possible

126

I was sad
Mad
Big things going wrong
Big
Asked for a miracle
Nope
Screamed for it
Nope
Then looked around
Miracles everywhere
Just not the one I so badly wanted

127

The rubber always meets the road
And I so often stumble when it does
I am a blunderer-er-er-er
Every time I get the tiniest bit righteous
It is just not allowed
I talk generosity
(Then argue with my husband about plans that take from my retreat time)
I give generously to others
(Then add it up as a debt to myself)
I don't join in on cruel talk
(Then I cruelly gossip about those who do)
I wonder how I'm even attracted to 'good'!

128

Depleted
Bored with my own searching
Staunch with disbelief I come
To the only place I find balm
My anguish begins to break
My kind of prayer
Regardless

129

Festering
Why this word?
Why not mulling
Or ruminating?
Why festering?
Hurts wanting out
That's why
A sliver
Can be lived with
Or taken out
Pull it out to heal
Will hurt to do it though—
Now I know why 'fester'

130

Woke to joy
There it was
Spread out in front of me
Now I could weep
Life intervened
A 'to do' list deflated my joy
Guess my joy wasn't strong enough

131

I have such hunger
I want to eat life up
Gobbling to beat death to it
Munching on music
Savoring weather
Drinking colors
Preserving laughter
Filling up on family
Such an appetite

132

We need a revision of our God image
Less father, more mother
More mystery
More softness
More compassion
More right now
Not past or future
Mama Now

133

Heal the harsh words from today
Between loved ones
What heart-hurt that is
Make the impact small
Let love weigh more than pride
Being right is a battle lost
Irrelevant to love

134

I ignore the world
It scares me
The hate is so big
And tangled together
Every string pulls another
Too tight to unravel
Fingers pointing everywhere but near
Not me—not now
I'll help later
Let me enjoy
Just a little bit longer
I don't want to look
Not yet

135

I can get so angry at fatuous affirmations
Let them pass the snicker test
Put them in the mouth of an Afghan cripple
Or a starving Brazilian living on refuse
Then let the words prove their worth
To bring about miracles

136

Busy busy busy
Goals goals goals
Fluttery mind
Get up
Go out and about
Go go go go go go go
I stay
I squirm
Peace almost
One more wiggle
Goals slide away
I sit
My part done
I wait

137

Compliments scare me a little
Afraid they ruin everything
Make me self-conscious
Piling up definitions of me
From the outside
Changing my inside
Confusing me
Knocking me off center
Afraid I'll chase the compliments

138

To think prayer produces results
Now there's an idea
Not just comfort or yearning as a last resort
But a force
Power beyond geography
Beyond time
Not mental shenanigans
Not willpower
But transforming energy
I call that awesome

139

It is so wonderful
To not care
Who or what
Wins the truth wars
Which only makes
Them the liars' wars
And frees me
To pray
My way

140

Too much coming at me
My chest is tight with resentment
As I smile
Hypocrite!
Give me grace to walk within my breath
Not ahead or behind
Regardless of the task

141

Well this sure puts my nose in it
A huge high-impact-God-awful death
Unexpected—accidental
The tragic kind
The car crash kind
"Peace that passes understanding"?
I think not
Try soothing this heart-branding grief
I know acute grief transmutes
Into livable sorrow
Who cares?
I know no comfort

142

I talk love
But I'm not so good to me
I hack away at my imperfections
Ruthlessly
But with no result
Because
They are not separate from me
They are me

143

Was wallowing a bit
Not seeing all the good stuff
My life is full
So rich
Full of learning
Creating, loving
Work
Who could ask for anything more?
Well, give me a minute

144

I want to right size my life
Shed some stuff
Pare down daily irritations
Make large the work that's mine to do
A medium size ego to make it happen
Lots of energy to do it
Few, but true friends
Less to heal
More to give

145

Peace has found me
I wasn't looking
But here it is
Warm calm
Easy breath
Joy building
Content
In harmony
Nothing needed
I don't move
Wanting to hold this place
That can be so easy-come, easy-go
The staying power of peace takes surrender
Tiny deaths of self

146

On a bad day
Too much mystery
Makes me nervous
On a good day
It all seems glorious

147

Well, divine
I am ready to cull
My abundance is waste
Of time
Of energy
Of money
Of lost opportunity for others
My soul's ecology doesn't work anymore
Time to give
To create compost for others

148

So grateful for respite from sorrow
Joy seeping in
So relieved that
Grief will not be my home
My heart is tender, fragile
But my soul
She's a worker
Sturdy
She stands ready

149

Could it be
That all the interruptions are my life
Not the sitting still blissful one I yearn for
But the chance to love in the trenches
Sooooo not retreat
So in it
So very in it

150

Gagging with sorrow
Stumbling through tasks
Whatever I touch
Crumbles
Nothing works
Know all will be better
At least different
I come beaten for the moment
Looking for comfort
Relief
I wait

151

I love the cosmos' sense of humor
Won't allow pious posturing
I decide to do devotions outside
On the porch
Perfect morning
New buds
Newly planted window boxes
Early spring orderliness
I settle in for gratitude
Centered, eyes closed
The jack hammer starts
Across the street
Invasive, unremittingly aggressive

My marriage ended—

—the usual stuff
I was surprised by the nice guy
An affair—an abrupt ending
A shredded heart and bewildered little ones
A wise therapist piecing me back together gave me a recipe for dark night despair:
One shot of whiskey, one Psalm and one thread on a cross stitch project
"If you still feel you can't live, call me"
I never made the call
But God was front and center again
With a capital G
Psalms soothed me
Prayer guided me to accept and forgive
Not as a victim
But to grow as a strong working single mama
Devotional reading kept me going
As well as irreverently humored friends and hurting kids who needed a functional mom

152

I am carbonated with joy today
My very cells are vibrating
With happiness
The—not very often in life—kind
A long-awaited baby has joined us
The miracle is here
A lesser word would be profane
Alle—unbelievable—luia

153

Give me a sincere heart
So true
It thuds to my feet
Locking me into place
Not grounded
But rooted
The deepest, downest
Me

154

Aware
Of my enjoyment
(OK—my need)
To be needed
To be right
An expert
Chosen as best
An old stance
Not needed any more
A youthful habit
And I'm not young
So poof
I can be and often am
Wrong, dumb, and not the best
Hurray

155

The world can be so noisy
No wonder monks built gardens
Takes more than a garden for me
I need a redwood forest
To quiet me

156

I have just had goodness dropped in my lap
A miracle maybe
Grace for sure
And still I don't trust goodness
Don't lean into it
Talk the talk but don't walk it
I honor fear more
Don't want to walk the fear
Let my DNA absorb goodness
When it comes my way
Kick fear out
Trust what's been given
See it first

157

I'm getting wiggly
Tasks call me
I want to get going
But I stay
Dig deeper
No time, no clock, no list
Be still, Wiggler

158

It's so very easy to forget about others
MY life
MY joy
MY pouty troubles
MY wanting
MY shallow caring
Much ado about nothing
Reverse my attention
At least for five minutes
A start

159

Shedding
Shedding things to do
Shedding feelings
I wait
Getting ready to receive
Praising
Listening
Praising
Thanking
Shutting up

160

I take my miracles small too
A walk
Spring still tidy and new
Every lawn mowed
Full tide as I walk the ocean path
Baseball shouts
A red flitting cardinal as my pal
Odd sorts of people
Beatific at the same time
Almost eerie
A diorama scene
A hint of wide spread harmony
Maybe not a small miracle

161

I want to wake up in joy
Live in it
Not build it fresh every darn day
Like an insult
To the universe

162

I'm praying for all the jerks in the world
The powerful jerks
The ones who make life miserable for others
And like it
Who think they know
Who scare with their rigid rightness
Who I prefer to hate
But try to bless instead
For them
For me

163

Yearning
I'm yearning
Almost all the time
Prayer, meditation, silence
Soothe yearning
Why would I forget that truth?
When
Again and again
Here is where yearning stops

164

I do believe I'm coveting
Wanting what others have or
Wanting them not to have it
A petty small place
Jealousy
I need heart expansion
A remodel
To make more room
For us all

165

You can't force faith
Fall into faith like falling into love
Jump
Relax
Let go
Muse
Slide
Sink
Allow it

166

Tonight I sizzle with ideas
With possibilities
With hope
With a sense of something at work in me
Propelled
Quickened
May it not be just a manic moment

167

When I go away
I go far away
Disconnected
Prayers seems a distant habit
Quaint
Superstitious even
And then
I begin to have a hankering
For something more
In the big fat midst
Of wonderful happenings
Yearning like a bad itch
That can't be scratched
And here I am again

168

Some hurts are such a long sore ouch
Grinding in the stomach
Neglect
Dishonor
Wrong blame
Malice
Meanness
Betrayal
These tear at me today
May I not ever do the same
Would I know?

169

On empty tonight
Tired of myself
Tired of thinking too much
Low spiritual ebb
If we knew there was no death
Would we care about the meaning of life?
We'd have to do something to make
Everlasting life bearable

170

Stuck in the posture of prayer
I've hit a skid
Off balance
Skittering to catch my balance
Nothing to hold onto
Sliding to a stop
The idea of prayer awkward and false

171

Bless all the angry people
Where do they all come from?
From other angry people
How dumb dumb dumb
Can we be?
Soothe just one hateful person
Today
Then pray for
A multiplier effect

172

Dare I ask for another miracle?
I am a bottomless pit of requests
Miracles like hail
Knock me down
And I dare disbelieve?
Even I know I'm not that lucky
It has to be miracles
This avalanche of good

173

Reading
Skimming
No traction
Words and words and more words
Written by others
None sit right for me
Tonight
No room for them
Already too full
Let the words settle into silt
To grow something later

174

My gluttony is so huge
(What else could gluttony be?)
I want to read every book
I want to taste every food
I want to visit every country
I want I want I want
When I have I have I have
So much

175

Interior life
Can get overly glorious
Let it be like
Taking vitamin C
Daily
Necessary
A nutrient

176

Untethering
Everyday a letting go
Of body as it deteriorates
Of old roles as children assume them
Of many friends for the essential few
Of stuff I love but don't need
Of wrestling with self
Untethered
I am who I am
Liberated
Free
Happy
Alone and full
Who knew?

177

Praying
Hooked on myself
Working to find peace for me
Then one phone call
One person to give to
Extending myself to someone else
And I am flooded with contentment

178

My life seems both long and short
Focus shifting
Past or future
Regret or yearning
My prayer is to shake off both
To stand in the now
Now

179

I snap at the universe tonight
Bitter
Mad as a hornet
Answered prayers
Yet leading to unexpected sorrow
Wanting
Getting
Regretting
Get me off this Ferris wheel

180

Even as I pray
I don't know
Anything
For sure
I accept that
Easily now

181

'God is too good to be true'
Isn't that the best argument?
For ambivalence
God?
Wanting the best from us, for us?
Guiding us to our purpose?
Knowing the hairs on our head?
Assuring another life after this?
Healing all kinds of wounds?
Too good to be true
Unless—

"First comes love, then comes marriage"—

—next comes divorce
And a second marriage
I followed the patterns of our times
A seismic upheaval
Moved from Illinois to Maine
New husband
His three children, my two children
Left all family and friends
Left two houses unsold
No one with a job yet
Three days before the start of school
All in shock
Forget devotions
I screamed prayers as I tap danced fast with too
much on my plate
My favorite white knuckled mantra was:
"I can do all things through Christ
who strengthens me"
Well, I couldn't, but that phrase kept
me going

No formal worship
My husband and I couldn't coordinate our
beliefs or our kids to get to a church
But under duress, I turned to God-ness
During good spells, not so much
Hardly fair or honest

182

I am an ingrate
I bask in a translucent spring day
All my loved ones are better than good
A rare moment of fruition
Still I dig like a pig
For truffles
For that dark gnarled clod
That blocks full joy
My prayer like a toy shovel
When a backhoe is needed

183

Overtaken by dark thoughts
So rife
I enjoy the fury
The mildness of optimism and faith
Irritate me today
There are such wounds
In our earth and in our chests
It is simpleminded to smile through them
Unless a very pure simple mind

184

You know that ancient hurt
That is now your best friend?
Give it up
Disintegrate it
Into little pieces
Blow them away
Like a dandelion halo
Poof
Gone
Doesn't have to be agonizing
Just a shift of the story
Go ahead
Side step
Shift

185

Send help now
I'm in a deep canyon of hate
Feeding on it
Gorging
Voraciously hating
Send help

186

Use all the comfort words you want
But I am afraid of dying
Afraid of death
Things have to get pretty bad here
To want death more than life
And THAT really scares me
I fail the test
I still think death has its sting

187

I've gone cranky
As a habit
Doing the opposite
Of all the affirmation stuff
Bitter even
At last I shift
Summer porch revival
Soft air, many blossoms
Wiggly birch leaves
Breathing deep
Melting brittle anger

188

What a good day!
I would say glorious
(If it didn't sound so trite)
Perfect weather
Easy deep connection with a friend
A triumph in my work
I would say delightful
(If it didn't sound so precious)
Playful time with my daughter and with hers
Affirmations for new direction
May I please please please
Remember
This does happen

189

Easier to believe in small stuff
Miracles in our individual lives
Why not scale up?
It's the world that's needy
We need global miracles

190

I do slack off with prayer
When things are good
I drift
Until a specific gratitude
Knocks me in the head
Shocking me with shame
At such
Thanklessness
Such forgetting
Of what it means
To be steadfast

191

A little less prayer
A little more action
I groan at the thought of
Extending myself
I've done my share
Can't I be just an elder
Dispensing wisdom?
The answer is—
No

192

Too well caffeinated
I start my day
Wondering what is joy
And what is jitters
Regardless
This is a day that quivers with
Mini-miracles
Backlit petunias
Bicycle wheels blurring
In the sun
Why do I see it so clearly today
And not on others?
No
Not caffeine
I won't kick this blessing in the mouth

193

Every time I come back to prayer
I feel nuts
For avoiding it

194

Trying to pray
I resist
I read one more devotion
Do one more email
Play online solitaire
Get squirmy
I give up
Shut up
And sit

195

Belief can become a giant 'should'
Or a way to get the goodies
I don't believe in that belief
I say, pray easily with pleasure
The experience changes over time
Trust emerges
Keep going
See what's true—for you

196

When I read Old Testament Bible passages
I wonder if God isn't self-centered
Demanding reverence
Or else?
Floods
Wilderness
Then along comes Jesus
All compassion
Master teacher
Of real heaven
For this lousy world
So, God evolves too
That's a comfort

197

May we save this earth
I forget the damage we do
Sitting in my own beauty
I can ignore
The damage
Of my plastic bags

198

The word 'God' is a spoiler
It takes mystery and makes it too narrow a metaphor
The Islam faith has 99 qualities, thus names for God
Christianity has a basket full
Can't count all the Hindu variations
Judaism never named the un-nameable
Any name trivializes awe

199

Sometimes
I find spiritual searching
Distasteful
Too intangible
Often smacks of
Charlatan
Vague words
Forced optimism,
An insult to true suffering

200

Prayer tastes good
Like the first bite
Of a favorite food
When you are hungry
But you don't get filled
You get hungrier

201

I am working hard to love less
Turning my energy elsewhere
When my love is not wanted
Which is actually
An act of greater love
More love or less love is the solution
But no more knife edge balancing

202

OK, what does 'not being' feel like?
Dying is bad enough
But 'not being'?
Whooooa
Cosmic sensory deprivation tank?
Forever?
Am I only memory energy?
I want the courage to look this all straight on
Open to any mystery
From playing cards after death with my mom
To being in the angel chorus
To resting as nothing
Gulp!
I laugh
No idyllic prayer today

203

I can turn so fast
From
Hating everything
To loving it all
And prayer is
The toggle switch

204

I can't stand the words
Of prim pious people
Basking in their spiritual glow
Nor over sensitivity to all secular
Nor denial of real world grit
Nor forced dumb optimism
Nor martyred giving
Nor a 'tsk tsk' attitude
Nor people hooked on sin
Nor highfalutin' love language
Nor spiritual language you can't stand on
I want simple honest words for my prayer

205

I want peace
I have been in pain
With worry about my kids
Their hurts are such big ones now
Adult children with
Their own prayers to pray

206

If everyone who prays, makes requests
Then you would be busy fulfilling orders
So hard not to make my faith quid pro quo
I'll believe 'if'
I need to erase my thoughts of a spiritual bank account
With debits and credits
Bless you right back God
With the beard
Amen

207

Numbing myself with distractions
Won't work
Not books, not food, not friends
From whence cometh my help?
"From Psalms, dear lady
From Psalms"
Doing what they're supposed to do
Praise and comfort and wailing
Yowling also allowed

208

Really?
A relationship with the divine?
Or me talking to me?
Words are a barrier
Mystery stays mystery
Even a metaphor can trivialize wonder
Ambivalence and awe
Confusion and awe
Still, awe

209

Thanks
Big thanks
A good day
So much paving the way
I love the daily help given
To small things

210

Writing prayers
Grounds them
Like a lightening rod
So they don't
Simply strike
And evaporate

211

A book title I remember
Suffering Is Optional
Clever
Not true
Suffering just is
Buddhists cool it way down
Neutralize it
Christians tend to fall in love with it
Sufis chase it away with ecstasy
Others affirm it away with positive thinking
I turn it to sorrow
And then sorrow to sweetness
An alchemy of sorts

2/2

Tasks or solitude?
Perpetual question
I sit
Knowing I won't for long
A blue jay perches two feet from me
I freeze
Normally, I don't care about blue jays
They get a flicker or less of my attention
Up-close
A different story
Up-close
Beauty
Detailed markings
Individual feathers
Ten seconds and gone
Speed prayer
Speed learning

Plugging along –

—getting kids through college
Enjoying them as adults
My parents die
Old, but still suddenly
Can that really be unexpected?
They die within a week of one another
Hearts just done
I trudge through my grief
Heavy like a dentist's lead vest
I need comfort
And it comes
In April with snow on the ground in Maine
Blooming pansies appear clustered
Paper plate size
My mom's favorite flower
Never ever planted them
I hated them—too grandma like
My dad's requested funeral song was Greensleeves—
it stalked me

Played in bookshops, the mall, the drug store
I knew it was comfort from my mom and dad
I did take the comfort
Chalked it up to weird
Plowed on

2/13

In mourning today
For my brother
Afterlife doesn't comfort me
Here-life hurts now
Having loved well is the only comfort
And not much at that
Punch in the stomach grief
It will pass
As we will too

2/14

Lift me out of my self-indulgent agony
I have First World mini-blues
Conflicting family loyalties
(How awful!)
Worry about adult kids' lives
(Oh no!)
Cataclysmic in my stomach
So minuscule in the world
Perspective
Where'd you go?

2/5

A Disney cartoon size bumblebee
Starts my day right
Doing the impossible
That body shouldn't fly
And does
Well then!

2/6

At the end of today
I berate myself
Mad at me
Mad at the world
I got lost in the day to day
You are not real to me
I'm stranded

2/17

I am hungry
Sated only on the divine
No, not sated
Hungrier
Words keep coming
Unable to accept silence
The only reasonable response is—
Sorry, words,
You are superfluous

2/18

Devotional words sicken me today
I scan and skim them
Wanting to land
To dig in
I do not want
A dark night of the soul
It's been so sweet for awhile
But I've heard they are mandatory

219

I've got to honor this day
For its flow and harmony
After days of bitter bites
Like a plague of itchy irritations
Then this day came
Smooth
Light
Loving
Easy
A stunner
I do believe
Grace is the right word to use
Thank God
I needed some

220

Sometimes joy does lift me
My heart wants to float
Ecstasy is right there
Just beyond my reach
So I quickly load my heart
With concerns
Not ready for full-power joy

221

Rather than make the phone call
Looking for work
For someone desperate
Rather than saying yes
To my husband to sit, chat
Rather than sending an email to
A bereft friend, I head
To my prayer place
Not knowing if one choice
Is better than the other

222

I don't want to 'join' anything
No book club
No theatre guild
No help-others-out groups
And no church
I don't belong anywhere
I hope the opposite is true too
I belong everywhere

223

I want hope
That dangles with joy
Sacred bling
Carbonated faith
Even as I sit quiet

224

Nature slays me
With or without God
It's impossible
Such perfection
Bewilderingly wonderful
A magnificent accident
Hard to believe
But there it is
Data

225

I let myself ring false today
Acting more love
Than I felt
Now that'll make
You soul sick
Fast

226

I have been cheerleading
Instead of settling into sadness
The situation
Calls for sorrow
And I have been
Bucking up
Cheering up
Pep talking
Maternal reflex maybe
Or my own fear
Probably

227

I trust my own experience
Not what I'm told
Not what I read
Belief
Faith
Hope
Come from my experience
I test
And then trust
Prayer
Is my continuing experiment

228

I have a place in my heart that hurts
When I love
Probably a scar
Protect it?
Or rip it open?
To finally heal

229

Real vulnerability
Is not at all like
Cute safe vulnerability
Of charming foibles
Oh, no
Real vulnerability
Is naked in front
Of enemies
Not for the faint-hearted

230

Such balm
Porch comfort
Crumbling wicker
Quiet devotions
A church Sunday
Not for me
I sit
And love God
Right here
Right now

231

Odd to be embarrassed about praying
Protective of my private life
And yet so many of us pray
Or say so when asked by a pollster
So many automatic assumptions pop up
Right wing anti-science
Liberal scorn
Atheist glee at dinosaur brain pray-ers
So much automatic wrongness
No wonder we're quiet about our prayer

232

If you mean business
Praying
Will change your stance
In the world
Don't get all happy
Get ready

233

Petunias in a lime green planter
With white polka dots
Make me happier
Than a grand mountain range
I can take it in

234

Of course I can be happy
With my soul out of whack
I love my bling
My grand kids
My porch
Pop corn
All life's goodies
But who wants to be only happy?

235

I have been awash in people
Fun, food, talk
Dishes, beds, conflicts
Summer!
Gone from stillness
So here I am
Ready for
Chiropractic for my soul
Silence

236

With this gratitude
I have to go to church
Need to raise a voice
With others
Ignore what I don't share in common
Glad for what I do

237

I breathe easily tonight
Happy for prayer
That aligns my
Insides
So that outside
Matters less

238

Deep gratitude
Starts high in the head
Awareness
Travels like
A trickle
Through
The heart
Rests in
The gut
And continues
Down to the toes
And out
Leaving
Deep grounded thanks

239

I've been doing some spiritual thrashing
Watching myself think about what is
unknowable
(At least by thinking)
The remedy is always the same
Get busy with gratitude
Out loud
Act for someone else's good
Up close

240

Bless us
The privileged
To know we are
Bless us
To shake off all the extra we have
Bless us
To trust generosity
To give
Not just until it hurts
But until it pleases

241

Soft
Summer air
Car tire buzz
Carbonated fizz of tree rustle
Bedraggled petunias
Mess on a summer porch
Frisbee, dead sparkler
All beauty
I have on the right glasses today

242

Sooth the ancient hurts of my family
Bring everyone
To the present tense
Fresh and ready
To enjoy all the good
And to spit
Out all else
Boom

243

Theological purity causes so many ills
Do you know
How many religious hairs can be split
In how many books
Over how many centuries?
Which came first?
Prayer or theology?
Experience or concept?
Natural reverence or rule-bound worship?
I honestly felt I couldn't have a prayer life
Until I knew what was true
I thought C. S. Lewis would tell me
Or Thomas Merton
Maybe ancient mystics
No such luck
Sometimes you just have to dive in

My husband and
I trudge along –

—sometimes flourish
Kids marry
Careers grow
Grand-babies arrive
Good adults with the problems of being adults
We have a far-flung but close family
Stretchy love
We ride up and down the waves with them
We retire sort of
We both write
We live part-time in Mexico
We read religion—all kinds—Sufi, Christian, Buddhist,
Hindu, Joseph Campbell-ism
You name it
We meditate alone and sometimes together
Faded hippies
We know we are spiritually thirsty
And wary
We and our doubts and our beliefs fit nowhere
Oh well, we say, oh well

244

I pray to change the world
Yes I do
I pray to change the world
One tiny drop of love
And reverence
Regardless of doubt
The world's ugliness
Laughing at me
Who knows the tipping point
Of one more prayer?
I pray to change the world

245

Yikes
I'm praying in a hurry
My mind flipping through
Images
Tasks
Unruly prayer
Intentions one place
Brain in another
Heart saying
What just happened?

246

Give me a pocket of peace
To face this funeral
With grace
To support those
On the front line of loss
Who don't yet know how
Loss grows
Before it transforms
Death is the easy part

247

Grant me respite
From being a jerk
I have a bad habit
Of bile spewing
Random anger
Laughable superiority
Cutting words
Indulgent mouthing off
Good for a sitcom
Not for
Daily living

248

I pray for heads of countries tonight
That they catch a glimpse of themselves
That they govern for the people
That they close their peacock feathers
That they be
Kinder
Nicer
More civil
Get better ideas
See a new model for living with all
See that very, very different is possible
Dare I hope?
Dare I not?

249

Thinking of prayer as experiment
Takes it out of the need
For perfect belief
Into experience
Silence is the starting point

250

I believe that something good could happen
Is happening
All acts of good count
All moments of gratitude lift everyone
All stretching to get to love strengthens us
All awareness of Now wakes us
All prayers add to the mix
Of something good happening

251

Lead me
Nudge me
I'll try to shut up
Guide me to the joy in today
Help me step over the irritations
Put me in my place
Growing the good
Silencing the bad
Firm on both feet

252

If I were to really step into my
Sureness about transcendence
(Code: God)
I'd have awful images to fight
Dowdy dour faces
Prissy mousy subservience
Dull plodding, slow hymn singers
Goofy spiritual babble
Overly enthusiastic fervor
Rigid rightness—enough to kill other people
Haughty meditators on their pillows
To name a few
And how about me?

253

Sometimes I walk away from prayer
With distaste
It's when I feel false—
Sincerity
Always brings me back

254

Modern religion has a problem
Of being bored with itself
Yadda yadda yadda
Droning hymn
Yadda yadda yadda
Stand up
Sit down
Yadda yadda yadda
Plowing through rote prayers yawning
Sermons numbing the minutes to frozen-ness
Yadda yadda yadda
No passion
No mess
No creative tension
No questions
Yadda yadda

255

I could pray the day away
And be in ecstasy
Only to awaken
And bite my husband's head off!

256

Opposites always circle around
And bump into one another
Then what?
Run the other way?
Play chicken?
Take a stand?
Meld?
Or let one another both exist?
Living on the same continuum

257

Morning prayer is the best
Fresh head
Soft heart
Hot coffee
Open to newness
Orienting
Choosing
A good day

258

What's up with me?
That's my prayer
I've been
Jealous
Negative
Nasty
Needy
Disappointed no matter what
Not out loud
Only my shadow knows
Perfect sunny weather
And my shadow's going nuts

259

My prayer machine
Is closed down
Out of steam
Inert
Waiting
Rusting
Needs a tune-up

260

Hate it
When I'm kind of nuts
And know I am
And still
I keep wobbling around
Bumpety-bump
Instead of holding still
And sinking
Into
Prayer

261

In the middle of contemplation
While letting go of greed
Accepting what is, as perfect
I get jealous as hell
Of people who get what they want
Easily
Entitled to it
Knowing they deserve it
Wanting that too
Boohoo

262

Bring me to the next good thing
Surprise me
With a new demand
Or just joy

263

Prayer makes me more interested in my life
More adventure, more possibilities
Not less turmoil
But a sense of more synchronicity and surprise
A storyline
Not all glory for sure
But more wonder-full
Even when depressed
What comes next
Is part of the story
The purpose
The arc of my life

264

Lousy prayer tonight
Fake
Feeling foolish
All arid and awkward
Ashamed at my naïveté
Bleh
Try a few rote words
And let it go

265

Remind me
Of the people
In the world
That would welcome
Like a miracle
Sitting on this porch
With comfort and coffee
The jackhammers at work
That make me rage
Would not even
Be heard

266

I am content
Many things seem right
Tonight
Still, I am
Ready for a stone
To be thrown
Into my pond
To disturb me

267

How odd that
Extrovert me
Craves solitude
Not to recover from people
But as my source
Like an electric car
I go only so far
And have to plug-in

268

Why wouldn't I pray for strangers?
Or every hurting person
Smiling their way
Through the day
When they
Want to cry

269

Prayers are like going to a great restaurant
It takes some effort to get there
Sometimes there's a wait
You have to pay something
For the experience
It works best
If you are ready to enjoy
Relax into it
Don't mind the cost
Part of the deal
Worth it
But, fast food prayers
Quick-prep suppers
Are prayer fare too

270

Prayer is not a head versus heart battle
Not brilliant brain versus sentimental heart
It's a soul thing
Where there is no war
Of any kind

271

I don't want to be dead
New physics doesn't soothe me
We're all energy?
So what?
'Not being' scares me
Taking another form is too 'science fiction'
A soul blob bouncing around in infinity?
Afterlife?
It won't be this life regardless
Maybe suffering will change my mind
But I don't want to be gone
Yet

272

Blessings from a window box
Doesn't take much
Misty alyssum
Neon pink petunias
Falls of pink tinged vine
Even the rain shredded lobelia
Every blossom positioned
Perfectly
Randomly perfect
No effort needed
Just right
Me? Or the flowers?

273

As my prayer deepens
I shut up more
I listen more
To subtleties
I'm happier when I'm sad
I'm tenderhearted more
And much more angry
At the world's foolishness

God doesn't give up –

—and does act in strange and wondrous ways (often the same thing)

All of our kids bring us to adventures

New places, new thoughts, new trials, new interests, new digging deep to understand

So, not unusual that our youngest daughter dropped us into a big experience

She is a Christian

How it happened, we don't know

One Thanksgiving she burst into the longest most articulate devout grace ever uttered

All eyes were open and roving with wonder (not the awe kind) as she prayed

She was twelve years old and had rarely gone to church—huh?

Much later as an adult, she finally found a church home that worked for her

She invited my husband and me to attend

Why not?

Another adventure
At the African Methodist Episcopal Church
(Trust me, we look like the Wasps'
we sort of are)
You can guess what happened
We both felt not just at home, but Home
Here was a place to be real and worship
Loud with joyous music
Quiet in deep private prayer
Real, real, real
Odd, odd, odd
We felt out of place and a deep belonging
At last
We got churned-up
Quickened

274

It must be so comforting
No, comfortable
To absolutely know
Your way is the right way
To have no questions
To allow for no subtleties
To call others wrong
To justify killing them

275

Right here
Right now
Shift out of the past
Shift out of the future
All those writers
All those wisdom writers
Were right
This is the 'it'
Make it good

276

Lost in my own drama again
Such a force
Farce actually
My little one-act play
One act
Wasted on foibles
Instead of
Something grand

277

This is getting serious
The words don't show up
But I do
Learning to like the mystery
Is weird
Unsettling
Uncomfortable
Tempted to retreat
But won't
I'll keep my discomfort

278

When I sit in solitude and silence
(Both are needed)
Sometimes my heart hurts
Maybe always
Letting it hurt
And staying with it
Is, for me, surrender
Letting go
Of this world's wants
To a freer space
Where peace is
Peace with pain
Joy with sorrow
That's the way it is
For me

279

Thoughts or feelings
Feelings or actions
Actions or belief
Which comes first?
God probably

280

Sometimes I think of
So many people praying
For different things
Different reasons
Different beliefs
And yet
All that yearning
All that gratitude
Circling around
And no tipping point
For peace
Yet

281

I run to prayer
From never-ending wars
From nature run amuck
From lethal illness
Not for cures
But for peace and praise
Anyway

282

Easy to fake gratitude
Make your list
From flowers to toilet paper
We can be grateful
Drone on
But
Go deeper to where it hurts
Try gratitude from there

283

Many people I know
Being battered by life
Lost love
Lost hope
Lost meaning
Why so many tested now?
Or is it tested always
And, always so many?

284

I like a sense of guidance
From
Let's say, God
It's soothing
Companionable
Practical
Unpredictable
Intriguing
I'll take it
Why not?

285

Sharing prayers makes me nervous
Exposing sincerity as a seedling
Ready to be trampled, yanked out
Withered by exposure
Get me back to the greenhouse

286

Skepticism doesn't cut it
Brings nothing to the table
Rationality
Is a fantasy
Quicksand seen solid
Mystery just is
You choose—
Enjoy it or not

287

We so matter
And we so don't
Which thought
Will I ride today?

288

I am embarrassed
By what my ego gets me into
When it deflates
I am chagrined
By the ego hangover
I have to live with
Thank goodness for humor

289

My soul is shriveled
Dry
Hardened
It refuses water
Could petrify
And join the world
Of petrified souls
Pretending to be happy

290

Compassion is what I have to give
To rampant haters
Writhing past the instinct
To hate back
Easier to do from far-away
Than up-close

291

No matter the book
No matter how holy
How wise
They have turned to gobbledygook today
Burning love?
Lifting up hurt as a gift?
Praise praise praise?
Gobbledygook
Sour sorrow wins tonight

292

My mind won't settle
It's too busy
Picking on me
This fault that fault
Pick pick pick
It doesn't know
My flaws are perfect

293

My soul got sick watching TV
Suddenly I couldn't bear it
Not couldn't—wouldn't
Everything felt contagious
Smirking violence
Evil conniving made funny
Juvenile women fighting
In thousand dollar shoes
All ugliness
I want beauty

294

I go to my comfortable bed
In cozy flannel
Scuffing along in soft slippers
Knowing I'll wake to good coffee
And food too
And to sun and hope
But with a stone in my soul
Because my privilege is not shared
Too many have no soft slippers

295

My nemesis
The car repair across the street
Knocking steel on steel
Hissing and juddering
Shuts down my silence
My prayer time
Now I hear cars on the near street
And dog tags jingling
Crows start too
Really?
Since when do prayers need a perfect setting?

296

Easy to get to a prayer place
Sit down
Shut up
Spill your guts
Get empty
Open up
Listen with more than ears
Give thanks
Go to work

297

Sometimes every devotional book falls flat
I speed through
Looking for something to slow me down
To hit home
I don't force prayer
Sometimes
I just shrug
And do some laundry

298

I come for comfort today
Boy, do I
Where do other people go?
When life hurts
After the mall and the ice cream
The too much wine
Internet titillation
Sex on the side
Where do they go
If not here?

299

Too many people I know
Know that they are dying
The rest of us are numb
Not awake enough
Not fierce enough
To see the glory now

300

Nothing worthwhile can be talked about
I'm sick of words
But struggle to come into silence
Chatter, chatter, chatter
Busy, busy, busy
Shut up
Leave me alone monkey mind!

301

Dear Mother
The world needs your
Mama-ness
To soothe and comfort
And calm
This fevered hysterical world
To remind us that
Peace can be
Harder to create than war
Peace is the true work of warriors
Women warriors

302

I have hit a dead spot
Prayer feels fake
And foolish
I miss the easy flow
I have 'prayer block'

303

I love feeling blessed
When it's so easy to feel
Beleaguered
And today
Here it is
Out of nowhere
I am blessed
And I know it

304

I hate daily tasks
Sooooo
I do mini-prayers
While emptying the dishwasher
I bless world leaders
While readying-up the kitchen
I bless friends and family
Folding laundry
I bless hungry children
Lifting up the energy
Of work that I hate
Into some kind of love

Returning to church after years and years—

—heated up my vacillation
Pray
Don't pray
Pray
Don't pray
So I had a choice
Pray only under duress and be a fair weather pray-er
Or give up all the searching and just try to be a good person
Instead, I chose to pray—anyway
Steady
Awkward
Self-questioning
Divine-questioning
Praising
Doubting
So—
I am no longer awkward praying
Or admitting to prayer
My kind of prayer, but prayer

305

I just stepped off my high horse
But, boy
Did I ride
Telling people who they were
And what they should do
Giddy-up ego
Shadow close behind
May I learn to walk the middle path

306

Many prayers
Are spontaneous utterances
Like a burp—
On suddenly seeing beauty
Or an internal cry
Of just too much hurt
Sounds
Of anguish
Of delight
Groans count too

307

Not everyone has this itch
This irritation
This curiosity
This lonely ache
This 'nothing's right'
In the middle of a really good life
That prompts a search
For the divine
Lucky me

308

Suffering is right smack dab in the middle of religion
How to tolerate it by focusing on future reward
How to numb it by feeling less
How to be indifferent to both joy and pain
How to glorify it so that pain IS the religion
How to affirm it out of existence
Be happy-happy-happy
Teeth clenched
What on earth to do with the pain involved in living?

309

Today
Prayer feels like a toothpick
In front of a train
Trying to reorient the world
Out of its hate

310

What if
Through all the babble
All the holy books
Battling one another
What if
Theology with its
Endless fine tuning
Of the rules
Of what's right
What if
Everyone
Shuts up
Holds still
And we all experience
The same kind of holy
What if?

3/1

Crows gone mad today
Sounds like it would hurt to caw that hard
Yelling back and forth
They screech my rage
"I can't bear the pain of this world
The violent DNA has to go
We can't keep gobbling up our earth"
I caw with the crows

3/2

Is God-ness emerging
Through New Physics?
So much is unseen
But at play
Let's expand
Our continuum of
What's possible
Evolving spiritually
Doesn't have to prove things wrong
Adulthood doesn't disprove the child

3/3

I want to admit to jealousy
There
I said it
Too bad
And true too
How human of me

3/4

Oh, world
Leave my solitude alone
No sooner said than my husband appears
Requesting this and that
Snicker-snack, our swords clash
Fighting to be left alone
I bite
He retreats
Soured solitude
I get up
To apologize

3/5

There is a thread of discontent
Running through my life
No matter how good
It irritates me
Like an itch in the middle of my back
I can live with it
But it distracts me
I create elaborate methods
To relieve it
My kind of prayer
Is the salve that finally works
When I remember

3/6

I have just discouraged myself
Off-putting conversations
Done wrong
Darts to the heart
Rather than heart to heart
Spontaneous is not always good
Healing needed

3/7

Spare me from cruel optimism
Let pain be pain
Not masking what is
Just allowing
Then thanking
Then joy joins the pain

3/8

Who cares about Big Questions today?
Who wants to wallow in issues of faith?
Of belief?
Not me
Not today
I want to get stuff done
Be foolish
Shallow
Funny
Live where life is
For today

3/19

Over-stimulated with play
First snow
New York Times Book Review
Blog fun
Facebook photos
Sequestered Sunday
Who needs prayer?
Whoa-whoa-whoa
Ever hear of alleluia????

3/20

I am sick-to-my-stomach sad
My family is far flung
The holidays wear me out
Too much work for not enough joy
Belonging nowhere in my beliefs
More life behind me than ahead
Pure sourpuss today

321

Why this constant ache?
My life is good
Yearning souls can be pesky
Have to feed them a steady diet of prayer
Seems to help

322

I surrender
Big sense of the word
And small
I give up
Getting it right
Making it right
Being right
Feeling right
Doing right
Let things right themselves
A cosmic shrug
Is needed

323

I pick on myself
Grinding away at my flaws
Trying to polish myself
To be a diamond
When lumpy bumpy coal
Is just fine
More useful

324

I want my family to be whole
And here
For Thanksgiving
All of them
Happily chaotic
Vital
Travel weary
I want them to want to be here
Still, love stretches beyond geography and holidays
I am an ingrate on Thanksgiving

325

A sacred moment
Right here
Right now
In the middle of chaos
A pocket of peace
A hint of infinity
Grateful again

326

I wrestle with the sounds of cars and machines
Mad at where I live
Noise in early morning
Supposed to be my time
Prayer time
Could stamp my feet
As if time and place
And noise
Could be a barrier

327

Thanks for this fermentation
This prying out of doubt
Out, sour victim
Out, patterns of defeat
Out, constant irony
Out, waiting for new hurt
Joy is knocking at the door

328

Humming with exhaustion
I stagger into prayer
Stumbling to arrive
Empty beyond empty
I wait
Collapsed
Frantic for rest and comfort
I bow my head and pant
Can peace come?
I breathe and breathe again

329

Listening
Wondering if I hear
Wondering how to hear
I hear cars
A phone
My chatter
I listen
I hear my pain
My gratitude
My joy
My fleeting moment
All of it
Too large to absorb
I listen

330

Chasing joy is a fool's game
Joy has to come to you
Let it

331

My circle of concern has gotten small
MY friends
MY family
MY hopes
MY ups and downs
What about out there?
People grinding their way through a day
People traumatized by violence hovering over them
People furious at unfairness in their life
People in the quicksand of depression
Sinking with no foothold
Widen my circle of concern
To care
Even if impotent to act

332

An hour-long meditation
Is not prayer
It is emptiness
Prayer is
Fullness

333

Am I a fraud?
A confused searcher?
An honest searcher?
At least searching
Why settle in one place?
Faith doesn't mean 'shut up, don't think'
I'll settle for not settling

334

I create a prayer closet
With my breath
Shutting the door on
Tasks
Clutter
Relationship worries
Goals
Failings
Just breathing
Until
Fullness strikes

And now –

—I expect to continue to pray
It will be different
Not the same as the first prayers were
Prayer has its ages and stages
I expect to talk more about prayer
As I come clean about its importance
Most family and friends find it
Boring or strange
And change the subject
But I am no longer mortified
To admit I pray
Isn't that an absurd transformation?
I intend to enjoy praying for the rest of my life
As the grandest of explorations
Of possibility
Of comfort
Of peace within turmoil
Of hope for a tattered world
To guide my purpose

And for hints of grace
Until I'm done here
And evaporate into joy

335

Giving too much usually bites back
Help me resist being the rescue squad
Instead
Let things sink or swim
Get me out of martyr mode
Suffering sucks
So does being proud of it

336

Right here
Right now
Guide my mouth
To call or not to call
To let things lie or stir them up
To speak my truth or not
There is more than my truth

337

I am afraid
Of pain
Of ill health
Of hurt to my loves
Of catastrophe
Of evil
Of craziness
Of destruction
How dare I talk of bliss or love
I learn nothing

338

I am mid-crisis
And rarely think of prayer
But I scream
"God help me"
Silently
Every moment

339

The peace
Of getting real
With my flaws
Letting those flaws just be
Transforms them
What flaws?

340

Mine are such normal worries
Expected
My pettiness astounds me
Me-me-me-me-me
Forget me
Bless those in true tragedy
Living in horror
Blessings on
The truly hurting

341

Do I make you up?
Are you my projection?
Then I am better than I thought
Because you are pure goodness
Not I
I am ego swaggering
Even in prayer
How would I ever conjure you up?

342

The world got here first
Requests
Phone
Guilt of things not done
Irritation
I stew
Do I give up?
Do I fake prayer?
Or let it be?
I sit in my kind of purgatory
Not in, not out

343

I have undone holiday tasks
Like a Santa bag of burden
I like to give, love to give
But the clock ticks
I am full of love not given on time
Cards not sent, words not spoken
Hurry up to give give give
Whoa, Nelly
Stop and receive
Pause for gratitude
Time opens up
Now, continue
Stay expanded

344

There are voices and books
That talk me out of prayer
Rather easily
Until I need it

345

Living with 'what is' is
Not defeat
Not submission
Not cynicism
Not anger
But peace

346

I'm watching myself pray
Which means I'm not
One prayer ruined
I breathe and begin again
Wending my way gently
To where I'm not watching me
Eye on the divine instead

347

I kind of laugh
About thanking in advance
For prayers answered
I get it
It's a vote of confidence
But to me it sounds like
"Put it on my card"

348

I pray and stop to mean it
To deepen the impact
I pray for
The cold people
No coziness for them
No goose down comforter
No new Christmas sweater
No hot coffee on command
Does my prayer right anything?
Is anyone warmer?
Prayer is sometimes too easy

349

I tried it all today
Reading a mystery book
Popcorn
Sitting by the Christmas tree
Fireplace blazing
Anything but sitting in my pain of the day
Letting it run its course
A divorce leftover brought me down
Healing pain rears its head
Refuses anesthesia
Ouch
The pain-to-peace-continuum begins

350

This is the day to celebrate
Almost anything
From pillows
To health
If you pause—
It's all
Unbelievably
Miraculous

351

Such self-centered prayers!
There is a world out there
Try that on
Soldiers on any side who want to be home
Exhausted moms
Defeated dads
Confused kids
Hungry, hungry people in a fat land
Try those lenses on

352

Sometimes I need an answer
An intervention
Not just comfort and joy with what is
A result
And fast
Why not?
All powerful?
Bring it on

353

Time alone
Quiet
Twitching some
Heading into my kind of prayer
A little solitaire first?
Maybe a magazine?
One more text?
No and no

354

Loss happens
Everyday little losses
Big Life Capital 'C' Changes
With gain, still loss
Loss happens
Fight it?
Go with the flow?
Surrender gracefully?
You pick
Loss happens
Breathe that in
There's truth

355

Suffering of all kinds today
From existential to allergies
Knocked down by death
Punched—hard to breathe
My brother, my sister-in-law
Three cousins
More
All in six months
And six months later
I can still get punched
Missing them
Knowing I'm one step closer myself
To mystery

356

The problem with prayer is
Once you get an eensy bit of a bite
Of peace that makes no sense
That does indeed pass understanding
It's worse than craving chocolate

357

Shame is out of style
Our self-esteem is locked-in
We are all soooooo wonderful and unique
Our consciousness of wrong
Is refused
How do we course correct then?

358

Hungry for the holy
Then I laugh
Big raucous
Snorting waves of laughter
Laugh at all of it
Follies
Foibles
Tragedy
Fumbling egos
For the being alive of it
There's holy!

359

God
I have been a judgmental
Unhappy, tale-telling shrew
And suddenly I see that clearly
Lesson learned
Why?
Because I got caught in my nasty voice
And I want the consequences lifted
And so I pray
Beg
I sweat
I get why religion builds in
So much forgiveness
I want some

360

What if I'm a mystic in sweats?
What if all I care about is loving the divine?
What if all else is secondary at best?
Never considered that
Stunned by the possibility

361

Is it the New Year?
So many regrets
My fast mouth
My dominance
My self-centeredness
My desire to be really really really special
My laziness in action for all my caring
Caring costs nothing
Heavy invisible burdens

362

I settle into silence
Nice sigh
Then spend the time
Checking for arthritis bumps
In my fingers
Must have been important to me
Some use prayer beads

363

The ultimate ego trip
Afraid of being ugly
As you die

364

Why call it doubt?
Why not call it mystery?
Why see limit?
So many boundaries
Are self-made

365

Pissed at the universe?
I pray anyway
Discouraged about belief in God?
I pray anyway
Feeling intellectually flabby by praying?
I pray anyway
Embarrassed about a need for faith?
I pray anyway
Distracted by ambition?
I pray anyway
Hating everyone today?
I pray anyway
Over-indulging to erase sorrow?
I pray anyway
Feeling guilty about wanting more and more?
I pray anyway
Lousy with loved ones?
I pray anyway
Lost dreams?
I pray anyway
Just too, too happy?
I pray anyway

AMEN

I trust 'trust'
Belief and Faith are such loaded words
I trust (as in lean into, have confidence in)
That there is reality beyond the physical
That we co-create our reality with our prevailing thoughts and feelings
That God is a positive creative energy to align with for purpose
That we are in transition from one form of 'religion' to a new Mythos
That we are all on the same path
Whether we know it or not
That we all suffer and look for pain relief
That silence and solitude course-correct the soul
Wordlessly
That we are in a fragile time in the world as old forms fall away and new forms are not yet here
That each act of forbearance and compassion helps
That being human and flawed
Demands humor and fun
There
That's a start

MY KIND OF PRAYER

(In case you were wondering)

Here's how I pray
What I love best
Is to sit with myself
(And coffee)
In the morning
(In a red mug)
Before I talk at all
I sit and sip
And then
I read from some of my many inspirational books
If they are arranged by date, I go to the actual date
I ignore any days I have missed
For all the non-daily, devotional books, I pick a random page number for the day
I scan several entries waiting for a passage to flip me into prayer mode
I follow my intuition
Some quote, some message, some 'something' will ring true
I get hit by a theme or a person or a feeling
I sit with it silently

The words sink in and I follow what they trigger
Joy, grief
Asking good for others—
Or for me
Stating my very rough truth or feelings
I pause to listen, to get a sense of guidance
Just a sense
Last, I name people for blessings
Then I am naturally shifted into gratitude
Praise
Acceptance of it all
Thankfulness
Then silence for as long as it lasts
Listening
Restoring
Thanking

I have a couple of familiar places where I sit to pray
One is outside on the porch on an old couch
The other is a loveseat in my den
No homemade altar, no candle, no special way to sit
I wait until I feel a little settled
I open my iPad and peruse my many inspirational books
I write my prayers when I am struck by a quote or a reading

The iPad makes it easy to write without focusing
so that I stay in prayer mode
Sometimes I'm surprised when I read them later
When I feel done, I stop
Usually there is no sense of time passing
But most 'prayers' take 20 to 45 minutes
No rigid routine
Morning is best
Night works
Never in the midst of a day
Three to five times a week
I know when I get a scratchy soul that it's time to
find time

Do I believe in God?
'Goodness' only knows!
I believe in God-ness
I am totally open to mystery
God is not knowable
How we find language about the divine changes
We are in a paradigm shift about spirit
Things usually fall apart before a new form
emerges
We are caught in-between
New language and thought is emerging

The sacred continues outside of time and our paradigms
I hang on waiting for the next wave of knowing

I pray to God
And I don't know who I'm talking to
No one does
Unfathomable
There are hundreds of names for God—
Qualities of God
That's the mystery part
I like to talk to a person
(Even when I know that I'm not)
So what?
Just feels cozier
More accessible
Substitutes for the word 'God' make me either cringe or giggle
Not that they are wrong—just awkward for me
Although at one point in my life (irritated with the holy)
I prayed to Dear Random Lady Luck!
Talking to my adult son, I asked if he prayed
He answered—
All the time, I just don't worry about to who—
That's my point

SOME BOOKS I USE

A YEAR OF MIRACLES

MARIANNE WILLIAMSON

A YEAR WITH RUMI

COLEMAN BARKS

A YEAR WITH THOMAS MERTON

THOMAS MERTON

DAILY DOSES OF WISDOM

JOSH BARTOK

ENTERING THE CASTLE

CAROLINE MYSS

JEWISH WISDOM FOR DAILY LIFE

MIRIAM CHAIKIN AND GABRIEL LISOWSKI

JESUS CALLING

SARAH YOUNG

LOVE POEMS FROM GOD

DANIEL LADINSKY

MIND YOGA

FLORENCE SCOVEL SHINN

MY DAILY PURSUIT

A.W. TOZER

LIGHT THE FLAME: 365 DAYS OF PRAYER

ANDREW HARVEY

OUTRAGEOUS OPENESS

TOSHA SILVER

PRAYER

TIMOTHY KELLER

SMALL VICTORIES

ANNE LAMOTT

THE BOOK OF AWAKENING

MARK NEPO

THE MESSAGE/REMIX PAUSE

EUGENE H. PETERSON

THE POWER OF MYTH

JOSEPH CAMPBELL

TO BLESS THE SPACE BETWEEN US

JOHN O'DONOHUE

ACKNOWLEDGEMENTS

For my brother, Ronnie, who talked theology with me from the time I was twelve years old to, literally, the day he died.

For my daughter, Megan, who read my prayers by chance and said something nice enough that I wrote more.

For Reverend Kenneth Lewis and the Portland, Maine Green Memorial AME Zion Church that gently but powerfully shook my soul awake.

For Ariette Scott who lifted this work from the mire with her diligence and intuitive artistry and who was a partner in fun, tears and productivity.

For Mary Cushman who writes exquisitely and who helped me through moments of giving up.

For my husband, David, who takes my work more seriously than I do and who knows and says when something is good or not—writer-to-writer love and more.

For my adult kids who get a kick out of whatever crazy thing I do and who are my living laboratory for a rich life—Megan, Devin, Kayla, Ethan and Joshua.

For best friends who were willing not to read drafts of the book as I wrote it, because I care too much about their opinion—Eileen Kalikow, Helen Roos, Bob Stapleton, and Liz Swenson.

For friends and early readers who responded to my various blogs so that I realized the fun of having readers and the need for dialogue—Cindy Castleman, Katherine Cauley, Carol Eleazer, Victoria Farr Brown, Judy Gagnon, Scott Harrison, Susan Howe, Norma and Glen Kanwit, Erik Lantink, Lisa Miller, Eric Sanford, Tee Seales, Mike Strout, Michelle Thorpe-Hayes, and Janet and Rob Welsh.

For their contribution to cover development—Ariette Scott, Robin Tara, and Ed Zelinsky who all had an imprint on the finished product.

ABOUT THE AUTHOR

Joyce Wilson-Sanford is a former Executive Vice President for a global company, The Delhaize Group. She now works as an executive coach and is the writer of three unique and diverse blogs, I Pray Anyway, CEO Note to Self, and Truth Burps which can be found at joycewilsonsanford.com. She has been a frequent keynote speaker and leader of workshops on innovation, leadership development, and large system change. Now, she turns to writing with the same energy and commitment that she brings to her professional work.

Joyce's work and point of view is global. Three years in the Peace Corps profoundly shifted her into being a world citizen. Her work as a global executive took her to Belgium, Greece, The Czech Republic, Romania, Thailand and

Indonesia. Now, Joyce and her husband live and work from Maine, splitting their time with Mexico.

Joyce's life has had its share of profound challenges and she has gone through many permutations of devotional practices including having none. She has lived the modern woman's life from stay at home mom to divorced single parent to step family working mom to Senior Executive. She and her second husband raised five children and worked more than full time. From the bumps and bruises of her life, she has emerged with a very real, engaging wisdom that she shares in this book. Joyce speaks the language of the spiritually independent and articulates the ambivalence of the growing group who are religiously disenfranchised. She brings a unique voice to all her endeavors and insists that life and work have meaning and spiritual depth (which automatically means fun and humor) in an easy and natural way.

46030947R00157

Made in the USA
Columbia, SC
24 December 2018